ROSES OF HOPE

P.65

True Accounts of Intercessions by

Saint Therese of Lisieux

ROSES OF HOPE

True Accounts of Intercessions by
Saint Therese of Lisieux

REBECCA FABIANO

Printed in the United States of America

ISBN: 978-0-557-11703-1

This book is dedicated to my dearest grandmother. She had unwavering faith towards St. Therese. It seemed as if she was praying a never-ending novena. She was never selfish, and always included everyone in her prayers. St. Therese truly showered my grandmother with roses. She would find them everywhere, in her car, in the mailbox, from family, and from complete strangers.

When my grandmother lost her battle with bone cancer, I was truly devastated. It was difficult preparing for her funeral. However, St. Therese made sure that my grandmother had the most amazing and unforgettable departure.

The funeral home director commented to us, that in all of his years, he had never seen so many flowers. They just kept coming. In fact, there were so many beautiful arrangements, that they had to open an additional room at the funeral home just to place the overflow.

I know that my grandmother was welcomed into Heaven and I feel her presence with me everyday.

Contents

Acknowledgements

Thank you to all who submitted a story for this project. Without your submissions, this project would have never become a reality.

I would also like to thank my mother. She was my biggest supporter of this venture. There was a time when I felt as if I had gotten in over my head. She came to my rescue and typed as well as helped edit each story.

Introduction

Remember that nothing is small in the eyes of God. Do all that you do with love. ~ St. Theresa of Lisieux

Saint Theresa (Theresa of Lisieux), 1873 - 1897, French Carmelite nun, one of the most widely loved saints of the Roman Catholic Church. Her original name was Thérèse Martin, and her name in religion was Theresa of the Child Jesus; she is known as the Little Flower of Jesus. The youngest of five daughters of a watchmaker, she became, as proclaimed by Pope Pius XI, "the greatest saint of modern times." At the age of 15 she was permitted to follow two of her sisters into the Carmelite convent at Lisieux. There she spent the remaining nine years of her life and died of tuberculosis.

Many miracles are attributed to her, but perhaps the greatest miracle connected with her is that she became known at all. A simple nun in an obscure convent, she was remarkable only for her goodness. The holiness of her life so impressed her superior that Therese was asked to write her spiritual autobiography. This has become one of the most widely read religious autobiographies. It is filled, as are her letters, with her message of seeking good with childlike simplicity. She exemplified the "little way" —achieving goodness by performing the humblest task and carrying out the most trivial action.

She was canonized in 1925, just 28 years after her death, and Lisieux has become a major place of pilgrimage. There are churches dedicated to St. Theresa throughout the Roman Catholic world, and meditations from her writings are read by many of the devout with the frequency of a manual of prayer.

She is often represented in art with an armful of roses, because of her cryptic promise: "After my death, I will let fall a shower of roses." In 1997, Pope John Paul II named her a Doctor of the Church. She is the patron of aviators and foreign missionaries. Feast: October 1.

"Saint Theresa." The Columbia Encyclopedia, Sixth Edition. 2008. Encyclopedia.com. (August 26, 2009).

Special Note

Contained in a few of these incredible stories, you will find reference to a publication called *Leaves Magazine.*

Leaves Magazine is published by the Mariannhill Fathers of Michigan. It has been part of the Church in Detroit and all of America since 1938. It promotes devotion to God and his saints by presenting: the personal spiritual experiences of its readers, their petitions and thanksgivings, lives of saints and other holy people, articles on timely spiritual topics and prayers and edifying poems.

Leaves Magazine also features testimonies of readers to the powerful intercession of Father Engelmar, in the hope that he will someday be canonized a saint. Father Engelmar of Mariannhill selflessly gave up his life in March 1945 while ministering to those dying of typhus in the Dachau concentration camp.

For a sample copy, write to:

LEAVES
P. O. Box 87
Dearborn, Michigan 48121-0087

or call (313) 561-2330

Chapter 1

Bouquets of Roses

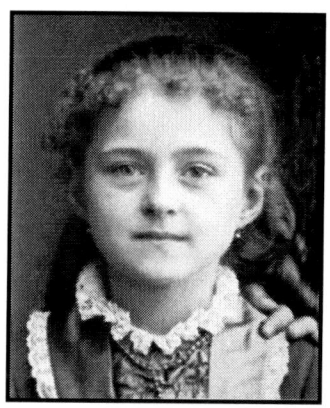

*"**L**et us see life as it really is...*
It is a moment between two eternities..."

~St. Therese

AMAZING ADOPTIONS

During the summer of 1980, Dennis and I were married. My sister had been praying a novena to St. Theresa when I met my husband-to-be. On the fifth day of the novena, Dennis sent me a bouquet of red roses. Dennis was Presbyterian and did not pray for miracles from our saints.

A few years ago, at Easter, Dennis joined the Catholic faith. He received his First Communion and Confirmation in the St. Theresa Chapel of Didde Catholic Campus Center at Emporia State University in Emporia, Kansas.

In the summer of 1981, Dennis and I started seeing doctors to help us conceive. Two years passed and we decided to get on the Catholic Social Services list for adoption. In 1984, we attended classes for nine months in Topeka for this adoption. There were six other couples also attending the classes. In the spring we began receiving announcements that the other couples had already received their babies. On June 15, 1984, I began the five-day novena to St. Theresa.

On the fifth day of the novena, I visited my neighbor, Frances, who was also Catholic. As I got up to go, I noticed that Francis had some roses from her garden in a vase. I commented on the smell and the look of the roses. Francis insisted I take the bouquet home. It was then I shared with her my novena wish. That same day, my husband was watching a show on TV and he called me into the family room to show me a bouquet of roses on TV. He then said, "I wonder if we are getting close to getting our baby?"

The next morning we left for a vacation to Branson, Missouri. After lunch we were tired and decided to go back to the motel and rest. A note had been taped to our door stating, "Don't leave, your social worker is trying to contact you." A couple of hours passed and she did indeed call. She asked us if we would like to adopt twin girls. Of course we were thrilled! We packed up, headed out of Branson, and drove straight to her house, arriving around midnight.

We named our twins Amelia and Ashley. The social worker told us they had not placed twins in over ninety years. I had been praying to the Virgin Mary and St. Theresa for another baby to adopt. Six months passed and on the morning of our twins' seventh birthday, I began smelling roses. I told my husband to get ready and that the lawyer would be calling any day. Around noon the phone rang and we were told to come and get our little girl, Annie Theresa. St. Theresa has been so wonderful to our family.

~Gloria – Kansas

EMOTIONAL PAIN IS ERASED

My husband and I were very hurt and upset because of a letter of complaint concerning me that my husband received from an executive committee consisting of three persons. We were not at fault, but we were not asked to tell our side of what happened.

I was deeply hurt, making myself very stressed and almost sick about it. I prayed for help to ease the hurt. Two of the persons involved apologized when we told our side of the incident, but not the third. We forgave them, even though it is hard to forget.

I would like the third person to apologize. I walk a lot and when I walk, I pray. I have made many novenas to St. Therese, God, and many saints for help.

One day before Christmas, as I was walking and praying, I said aloud, "St. Therese, when I come home, please let me find at least one rose petal from you to show me we were not wrong and to ease my hurt."

Sure enough, when I came home, a beautiful centerpiece was on the kitchen table. I looked for a rose and there were three beautiful roses tucked in with the other flowers. They were from a very dear niece and godchild. She had never before sent us flowers at Christmas, always before it was a personal gift.

I shared all this with my husband and thanked St. Therese. I called my niece to tell her about what had happened. I still can't say thank you enough. The pain of hurt has been erased. I have kept one of the roses as it dried. It's so special.

Love and pray to God. Pray to all the saints, especially St. Therese. They are in heaven helping us if only we ask. God bless all who read this story.

~T. M. – Ontario

ARTIFICIAL ROSE BLOOMS

At age 61, my mother had breast cancer and had surgery for a radical mastectomy. I made a novena to the Blessed Mother saying I was not ready to lose my mother. At the same time, I also was praying to St. Therese. After her surgery, while buying groceries at the supermarket, I purchased some yellow artificial roses to give to my mother. As time went by, these man-made rose buds seemed to actually bloom and open up! Mom lived to be 89 without any recurrence of breast cancer.

~Nancy – Pennsylvania

SOBERING EXPERIENCE

Since I've been a teenager I have had great love and devotion to St. Therese. On many occasions, too numerous to mention, I have had bouquets of roses given to me at the end of the five-day novena, even from non-Catholics who never knew I was saying a novena or ever heard of St. Therese. But the following is truly a miracle from dear St. Therese.

It was in April of 2000. My son, who is an alcoholic, was regressing. My husband was preparing me for the worst. As always, I was saying the novena to St. Therese (as I did every morning on my way to work). This particular morning, which happened to be Holy Thursday, I begged and pleaded with St. Therese to send me a miracle – to help my son see the light and go for the help he needed. Tears were streaming down my face as I begged to St. Therese to send me a miracle.

Well, that night, my son was brought to our house and entered the clinic the next day, which was Good Friday, and also my deceased dad's birthday. This was truly a miracle! He had been drinking for 20 years and was unable to stop. I told him the story when he came out of the clinic and he could not believe it and as he himself said "Ma, that is truly a miracle!"

He is a recovering alcoholic now and I still pray to St. Therese to keep him sober.

St. Therese is my pillar of strength. She has been through the years. I rely on her for everything. I also receive roses from the Carmelite nuns here in Massachusetts. I never know when they are coming but it is always at the end of my novena. I have given St. Therese's novena to many.

~Janet - Massachusetts

TRUE LOVE IS FOUND

I want to publicly thank St. Theresa for sending "yellow roses" showing our Lord's presence with our daughter, Teresa. Teresa was hoping and praying to meet her future husband. She knew that the Lord would hear the secrets of her heart (Psalm 37:4). I prayed for her to St. Theresa with the intention that St. Theresa would send a "yellow rose" to reassure our daughter of our Lord's answer to her prayers.

Shortly after, our daughter did receive yellow roses from a new boyfriend. He said he didn't really know why he picked the color yellow but he felt the red and pink roses just didn't look right. So he bought her the yellow roses and

Teresa was very touched to know that the Lord was truly personally present and that this new friend was more than a friend by chance. Needless to say, there continue to be many instances of our Lord's presence in their relationship. They became engaged soon after. They are thankful to St. Theresa and so are we. Most of all, we are thankful to our Lord for His constant care and protection.

Teresa and Joe were married July 6, 2002 at St. Robert's Catholic Church. Yellow roses were the theme of the wedding. The priest told the story in the homily at their wedding mass. Saint Theresa received a lot of attention at the wedding. Hopefully, this drew others to St. Theresa and her strong intercession with our Lord, ultimately giving Jesus all the praise and glory. Teresa and Joe had their first child August 20, 2003. Her name is Grace Marie. They continue to pray together and are showing Grace how to pray and how to make our Lord a priority.

~*Mary – Wisconsin*

SON'S SPECIAL DELIVERY

I am very devoted to St. Theresa and have been praying a perpetual novena to St. Theresa for healing. I had surgery for cancer in February of 1992 and started a novena to St. Theresa for a healing. After my surgery, my son came into my room with a dozen long stemmed red roses in a crystal vase. He did not know I was praying to the Little Flower. I saved every petal and put a statue of St. Theresa near the vase with all the rose petals at her feet.

In October of 1996, the same son, had five toes amputated on his right foot because of diabetes. On his I.D. tag he also made a medal of the Little Flower. Whenever we have a problem we always say "Pray to Theresa." My son is fine and I am in remission.

~*Mary – Ohio*

LOVE OF TEACHING

For many years, I have prayed the five-day novena to St. Therese. Early on, she impressed me with the power of her intercession.

I wanted, and needed, very badly to teach summer school in the early '70's. Since, in those years, teachers were chosen on a rotating basis and it was not my year, I realized that I probably would not get this opportunity. However, I prayed to St. Therese with this as my intention.

Summer school started, I had heard nothing. On the second or third night after the start of my novena, I hosted a dinner party and a woman brought me a huge bouquet of roses. The next day, I received a call to teach. I made the connection at once, of course.

In the fall of 1978, I suffered a heart attack and had to have a triple bypass. The night before surgery, two nurses, who entered my room separately and each at different times, asked where I was keeping the roses – that the room was filled with the fragrance of roses. I smelled nothing but I knew the operation would be a success and it was. I had absolutely no more heart problems until the summer of 2002, which was 24 years later. Glory be to God for his goodness and glory.

~Robert- Arkansas

ONE MORE CHORE BEFORE I GO

My mother was terminal with cancer and had a horrible summer (We didn't get along at all.) She stated "I wish I could can my tomatoes just one more time." So I started the five-day novena to St. Therese and on the fifth day I received three long stemmed red roses from my boyfriend and within a week my mom was out of bed (which she hadn't been in weeks), picked tomatoes, and canned them. It was the last thing she did before she died.

My boyfriend had never sent roses before or since. (That was a miracle to me!)

~Jean – Iowa

ONLY YELLOW WILL DO

I always asked St. Therese for a red rose whenever I prayed a novena for her intercession. But this time, I asked her for a yellow rose so I could be sure it was an answer from her.

Shortly after, my daughter, Mary Ann, got very sick with a colon problem and I went to stay at her house to help take care of my granddaughter. I stayed for three weeks and as I was leaving, a florist truck pulled up to her house. I went to the door and accepted a beautiful bouquet of 12 long stemmed yellow roses for her. When I brought the bouquet to Mary Ann, she said they were for me as a thank you for helping her and her family. When I asked why she had ordered yellow roses, she told me that she knew I loved the color yellow but the local florist didn't have any yellow roses. Mary Ann told them the roses had to be yellow so they went to a nearby town to find them. I knew immediately that they were my answer from St. Therese.

~Muriel – Virginia

I CAN HARDLY BELIEVE MY EYES

It all started when my husband got laid off from work. We had two boys still in school, a house payment, and a car payment. The first prayer I recited, I found in an article from Leaves Magazine. We decide to give it a try. We continued to pray, my husband was able to find work, but it was only part time.

We did not give up. Sister Mary, a nun, heard of our great devotion and gave us a beautiful picture of St. Therese. It still hangs on our bedroom wall.

My husband was out of work for nine months before he finally got a job. Just before my husband was hired, we received some beautiful roses from our friends for our anniversary. Then came the greatest gift of all.

I would go into our bedroom and knell by the bed and pour my heart out to St. Therese and to Jesus. On my bedroom wall appeared the most beautiful rose, full petals, and below it, a smaller stem rose. It was mostly an outline, but it was very visible. I asked a friend to come and look at it to see if she was able to see what I was seeing and she said she could. I couldn't believe my eyes! The rose and smaller rose stayed on the wall for many years.

Needless to say we were very grateful as our unemployment benefits were running out and we were paying our own insurance.

~Name withheld

RESTORED HEALTH

Seventeen years ago I was diagnosed with Multiple Sclerosis, and today I am very healthy. I no longer show signs of MS. I have a statue of St. Therese that I keep in my room. I can't explain it, but I feel her presence because I have received so many roses.

~Josie - Toronto

ST. THERESE IS ALWAYS WITH US

When I was 14 years old, I had a nervous breakdown with what was then called St. Vitus Dance. It is a disorder that occurs in children and is associated with rheumatic fever.

At the time, I was working in a factory and I kept dropping things, crying constantly, my tongue wasn't working properly, legs were flopping, etc. My mother took me to the doctor and he said that he didn't have any medicine that could help me. I had to help myself. As we went home, my mom asked me if I had understood what the doctor said. I said I did.

Mom started to make the novena to St. Therese at 3:00 every Sunday at St. Mary's Church and asked to make me well. I made the novena too, asking St. Therese one Sunday to make me well. I fainted while praying at the novena and the priest came to me and asked if I had gone to the doctor. I told him what the doctor had said. The priest said, "I will get you some medicine" and brought it to my house. I don't know what it was, but I did get better. Then I got rheumatic fever, however, I suffered no aftereffects.

So much has happened to me. I can't tell you of all the times I have called on St. Therese and all the roses she sends me in the oddest places. She is always with me. I have St. Therese and roses all over my apartment and many people have turned to her because of me. I am now 87 years old and feel I am never alone. Our Lord and St. Therese is always with me. I am so grateful to my mom for sending me to the novena.

~Ann - New Jersey

AT HOME WITH THE LORD

When my mother died in June 1983, I started a novena to St. Therese, asking for a sign if my mother was in heaven. It wasn't long after, that a co-worker of mine (who was unaware of my novena) brought me some beautiful roses from her garden! I truly believe that my mother is enjoying everlasting peace in Our Lord's presence.

~Lorraine – Florida

THE CARE MOM NEEDED

A few years ago, my mother was diagnosed with Alzheimer's. After a year or two it became necessary to find an adult daycare facility. Once my mother was all settled in, she didn't feel comfortable with her new surroundings. I was worried because it was a very good place with loving caregivers.

I decided to try to locate her to another facility, but it was booked up. We were placed on a waiting list and we patiently waited. One morning, while making my bed, a beautiful greeting card slid out from under the bed. It had a very large, red rose on the front of it. I got the card sometime before and must have saved it. I picked it up off the floor and I knew it was from St. Therese. I had a continuous novena going on to her.

My mom was able to get into the adult daycare program we wanted right away and she loved it. A few months later, she got sick and I prayed again to St. Therese. I walked into her room and there on the floor beside her chair was another beautiful card with roses all over the front of it. I knew then, that she would be all right.

A couple of years passed and my mother became very sick and we knew her time with us was very short. I prayed and cried and prayed some more. On her last night here, a niece came into her room carrying one dozen yellow roses. I knew mom was leaving us and it must have been St. Therese's last earthly gift of roses. Mom passed on, but a whole dozen beautiful roses from St. Therese must have been an answer to my prayer that all is well and she is coming to Heaven with me.

~Barbara – Massachusetts

Chapter 2

Glorious Rose Bushes

*"**B**e not afraid to tell Jesus that you love Him; even though it be without feeling, this is the way to oblige Him to help you, and carry you like a little child too feeble to walk."*

~St. Therese

WINTERTIME ROSES

My friend Carmella could not have a baby. The doctors told her there was no chance of her ever conceiving. So she decided try in vitro fertilization. Soon after the procedure, her husband bought her a rose bush and it bloomed during the cold winter. She now has a beautiful son named Matthew. He is truly a miracle boy.

~Josie – Ontario

MEDJUGORJE MEMORIES

It all began when my daughter invited me to go with her and her girlfriend on a pilgrimage to Medjugorje for our Blessed Lady's Birthday (August 5, 1989), which we departed for on July 31, 1989.

Because I had never been on an airplane and was afraid to get on one, I turned to my favorite saint, St. Therese, and prayed to her for special guidance - if I should go on this journey to Yugoslavia. After much daily praying, I received an answer.

One morning as I was cleaning and looking out of my front window, I spotted a beautiful rose on my rose bush. It was the only rose on the whole bush and I had not seen it there the day before. What made this rose so unique was the fact that I never saw that particular shade of color before. I knew then, that this was the answer for me to take the trip to Medjugorje.

When I prepared for the trip, I was no longer afraid and I felt complete calmness. This peace of mind lasted all through my trip and I really enjoyed my first plane ride to the beautiful country of Yugoslavia. We met some wonderful people from all over the world and enjoyed attending mass at St. James Church, where we sang and heard musical hymns that still linger in my mind. How sweet it was, hearing everyone sing in his or her own language, the same song.

We had perfect, comfortable, sunny weather and it was pleasing to walk and ride through the narrow roads and see how the people lived and worked. There were many grape vines and gardens filled with tomato plants.
While my daughter and her girlfriend were climbing Apparition Hill, also known as Mt. Podbrdo, I sat on a bench outside of St. James Church. As I waited for them to return, I saw the sun facing on top of me and saw it shine with surrounding beautiful colors. It reminded me of a pinwheel! The woman that was sitting next to me on the bench made me understand it was a good sign by placing her hand on my lap because she did not speak English. Also, when the sun was shining, I found it impossible to shield it from my eyes because I could not move my hands to my face. It was a great feeling.

Until today, I can't believe that I got to ride on an airplane and left my home and country for a very special pilgrimage to Medjugorje. I am most grateful that I went on this trip and that I did not disappoint my daughter and her friend. I will always cherish the many fond memories until I pass on....

~Story submitted By Dolly on behalf of her deceased mother, Grace - New York

HEALTH RESTORED

It was 1975, and I was at work in Northern Illinois when I received a call from my brother in Louisiana. He told me that our mother was very sick and not expected to live and I was to get home to Louisiana right away. While leaving work, a lady told me to pray to St. Therese and I prayed all the way home. I also prayed all night in the hospital while I stayed with my mother. Early the next morning, my aunt came to visit and before she left home she picked the last red rose off her rosebush to give to my mother, which she said she felt she just had to do but did not know why. When she handed the rose to my mother, I felt a chill go through me. When the doctor came in and made his morning visit, he was surprised that mother's vital signs were normal and she continued to get better every day. Mom lived three more years.

~Lena – Illinois

SUCCESSFUL SURGERY

On September 25th, 2001, my husband had open-heart surgery and had a triple bypass performed. I had been praying to St. Therese for a successful surgery. On the Friday before his surgery, my great granddaughter, who was then seven years old, brought home a rose she had made in school, with a love message. On the same day, my son brought me beautiful roses that came off his rose bush. I knew that St. Therese had answered my prayers and my husband's surgery was successful with great healing which he is still enjoying.

~Elaine - New Mexico

THE ROSE BUSH

Thursday

H ere in Florida, we have a rose bush and an allemande vine growing next to the trellis in the front yard. Roses generally do not grow without a great deal of care in this climate. Ours seems to survive everything. After the recent hurricane, the allemande was torn from the trellis, but has survived. Today, I saw what used to be the rose bush. It is now one stalk, about five feet tall with a single rose on it. This is amazing to me. I think that St. Therese is in charge of it and uses it to tell me that she is near.

Frequently, when I am worried, my husband will bring in a rose from this plant. He has no idea that I've been praying, but I think that St. Therese does and tries to comfort me to say that everything will be okay. And it is.
So, yesterday I said to her that I would send you this letter if my husband brings me a rose in the morning.

Friday
This morning he had brought in the rose and put it into a vase on the kitchen table. Therefore, I think that St. Therese wants me to send this to you.

Her knowledge is like that of a person who is looking out the window of a tall office building and seeing the cars below. From the position of the cars, he realizes that one car is going to be hit by another, as though he can see the future.
So it is with St Therese. She can see what problems I might encounter and tells me that she is with me always.

~Eileen – Florida

ROSES IN THE COLD

I n 1981, my son David, who was then 28 years old, was cutting wood for their fireplace with his brother Mike and a friend in the mountains of Colorado. As a tree fell, part of the tree hit David in the head. They were 60 miles from Denver hospital and it took a long time for them to reach the hospital.

He lay in the hospital for about a month. And for the first seven days he was unconscious. His doctors said there was little hope for David, if he lived, he would be the so-called vegetable.

When I prayed, I asked St. Therese to either please take him home or make him well. At the time, he had a wife and a one-year-old son. I asked her to talk to God for me. It was mid-November in Denver and David's wife, Brenda, and I were visiting her friend's house. It was cold and as I walked out onto their porch, where a rose hedge grew, a branch caught my leg. When I looked down there were two small roses and one rosebud. I called to Brenda's friend and asked if I could have the roses. She said, "This is November, if there are roses growing there now, you can have them." I picked them and still have them on my wall in a frame here in North Dakota. And I just knew by Thanksgiving, we would have an answer to our prayer.

The evening before Thanksgiving, my son opened his eyes. It took a year before he was allowed to go back to work. He is well and he can see, hear, walk and talk. He is a little hard of hearing in the ear on the side of the head where he was hit. He now lives in Michigan.

~Mary - North Dakota

GIFT OF FERTILITY

My sister and her husband had been trying for three years to get pregnant. She had been going monthly to the city to get hormone shots. When that didn't work, she went on a fertility pill for a while. Again, she had no results. Finally she stopped everything and gave her body a rest. I prayed to St. Therese.

In October, I happened to be out in my back yard. I looked at my rosebush, which only blooms in July and there was one solitary rose on it. I knew it was from St. Therese. And, of course, my sister got pregnant. Since she now had her gift of fertility back, she had two more babies in the next three years. Praise God!

~Eileen – Ontario

MONEY IN THE MAILBOX

Around 1980, we lived on a farm in central Iowa and times were quite hard. On a very cold December day, I was walking to the mailbox - asking St. Therese to help us. I looked back at the house and on the west side was a rosebush and to my surprise a big cream colored rose was on it – in December! I looked twice to be sure.

As I got to the mailbox, I reached in and there were several pieces of mail including one from Missouri. Back at the house, we opened the letter and out dropped a check for $30.00, from a bill over 30 years old. Don't say that St. Therese doesn't answer prayers!

~Christine–Iowa

Chapter 3

Solitary Rose

*"**J**esus, help me to simplify my life by learning what you want me to be - and becoming that person."*

~St. Therese

A HOME IS SAVED

My husband and I started having financial problems soon after he was transferred for his job. He had to take such a large cut in pay, that we were in the process of losing our home. I started saying a novena to St. Therese.

I work in a bank as a teller and frequently take my black prayer booklet with me. On the same day I started the novena, a customer sent me a rose in a canister at the drive thru window. I was shocked when I opened my prayer book and there was a picture of a peach rose identical to the one the customer had just sent me. My friends were also shocked and could not believe it. St. Therese is always there for me, answering my prayers. We got to keep our home, thanks to St. Therese.

~Mary – Texas

A ROSE AT MY FEET

I have great faith in St. Therese and have received red roses so many times thru her.

My son, Michael, had always donated blood at the blood clinic that was held regularly. On one occasion that he went to donate, they tested his blood and said he had a type of leukemia that attacks the brain.

This news was terribly hard for me since my husband was an invalid and I took care of him. I made a novena to St. Therese and on the fifth day of my prayers I attended mass. As I entered the church, there, at my feet was a single rose. I took it home and it bloomed for so long with such a beautiful fragrance that people would remark at how lovely it smelled. I told Michael that all was going to be well.

Later that year he had blood work drawn and sent to an Ottawa Clinic. The report came back in December – all clear! I knew when the flower was at my feet that I had nothing to worry about.

So many times St. Therese has answered me with a rose.

~Virginia – Canada

RECONCILIATION

I started praying a novena to St. Therese in 1993. I was recently divorced and soon realizing that it was a bad choice. I wanted to reconcile with my then ex-husband. About two weeks after I said the prayers to St. Therese, my two-year-old son brought me a rose that had been sitting on a desk in a chiropractor's office. He sweetly told the receptionist that he would like his mom to have that rose. The staff led him into the room that I was waiting in and he held up the rose to me. It was about 14 months later that my husband and I were reunited. We were civilly remarried five years after that.

Everything seemed all right when my spouse unexpectedly left and wouldn't return. He was soon involved with another woman. I asked St. Therese to bring him home, that he would quit drinking, and begin to see the other woman for what she was.

In March of 2000, I was walking to my car in a motel parking lot and when I looked down, there was a single pink rose with lady's breath around it. It was a boutonniere type of arrangement that had probably fallen off someone in a bridal party, but there it was at my feet. I saw many roses that year when I said the novena.

In July of that year my husband wanted to come home. I refused for a few months, not sure he'd mended his ways. During late fall, I asked St. Therese to show me roses if it would be in my best interest to accept. I was in a restaurant in November and there was a small bouquet of roses on the counter. My husband moved back home in January of 2001. He has been faithful and sober, thanks to God's grace and AA, since October 2000. St. Therese is so good to me.

~Janet –Illinois

SAFELY IN HEAVEN

About 20 years ago, our three month old granddaughter died suddenly of SIDS. I needed a sign from above that we would see her again. Days later, I went to the cemetery and there I saw a lady carrying a couple of roses with her. Not good enough, I needed a better sign.

When I left the cemetery I went to our son's home. There was the same lady with her roses! One of the roses was for the baby's mother and the other for me. Yes, we will see baby Sara again. She has the biggest job of all our 20 grandchildren. She is with all of us to help us get to heaven.

~Marlene – Minnesota

A ROSE FROM A STRANGER

I am 82 years old and was very young when I turned to St. Therese. Someone had sent me a *Leaves Magazine* and I was reading about the Little Flower and said to myself "this isn't real" and threw the magazine in the trash. Soon after that, my young son came in the house with a rose.

I asked him, "Where did you get that red rose?" He replied that a lady drove in our yard and said "Please give this to your mother."

I retrieved the *Leaves Magazine* quickly from the trash and drove to the St. Mary's convent in Penchory. When Sister Marjorie answered the door and I relayed my story. She said, "Thank you, you have made my faith stronger." Needless to say St. Therese has been with me all these years since we first met long ago.

~Norma – Michigan

A CHRISTMAS EVE TO REMEMBER

A bout five years ago, my son, Robert, suffered from a problem that was quite unique. He had difficulty swallowing and the acid and bile would constantly come up from his stomach. It had damaged his throat so badly that it was bleeding. He found a top gastroenterologist in New York who treated him, but to no avail. He was living only on creamed soups and losing weight every day.

Then Robert heard about an operation that would affect a duct going from his stomach to his esophagus, however, the operation was irreversible. I stormed the heavens. I begged St. Therese, St. Monica and St. Joseph for help.

When he went to another doctor for a second opinion, this doctor discouraged the surgery. I continued to pray and cry many tears. It was just before Thanksgiving and I pleaded that he would be eating by Christmas Eve.

One morning, I was walking to the trash bins in my condo complex, lo and behold, there lying on the ground was a beautiful artificial pink rose. There was no one around. I was in shock as I picked up the rose and cried. I knew my prayers had been heard.

Robert was given a new medication and improved every day and he was eating at our Christmas Eve dinner. I thank St Therese and all the saints every day.

~Gina - New York

A SOLDIER COMES HOME

A few years ago my son Ricky joined the Navy and was deployed overseas. They gave him a date that he was to return home. Later, they kept moving the date back, so I prayed my novena to St. Therese. I work in a bank at the drive thru window, and a lady that I hardly knew, brought me the biggest, red rose and sent it to me through the canister at work. Sure enough, my son got to come home on the Feast of St. Therese. St. Therese is the light of my life!

~Mary – Texas

POCKET WITH A SURPRISE

In the 1990's my husband retired on not so happy circumstances with the company he had worked for over 30 years. Although our children were all now living at home, or near us, my husband decided to move to Wyoming.

We had a "for sale" sign on our lawn and a garage sale. This broke my heart to leave my children and grandchildren behind and to be moving so far away.

My heart was heavy during the garage sale. I had to walk around the block hoping I could make it through the day. While walking, I prayed to St. Therese, please give me a sign that this move is going to be okay.

When I got back to the house, a car screeched its wheels and stopped. Two girls got out and they saw that I had a black tuxedo that my husband evidently took out of the closet and put on the line for sale. They wanted the jacket to go with her skirt for the prom. So I said, "okay, I'll take $5.00." I went through the pockets first and pulled out a beautiful bud rose. Evidently, it had been in there from past years when my son wore the tuxedo.

I feel my dear St. Therese came to my aid that day, to help me get through this very stressful time for me.

~Phyllis – Wyoming

HAPPY TO HAVE MY FEET ON THE GROUND

I had visited my daughter in Albuquerque, New Mexico and upon leaving Albuquerque to fly home, the plane we were on sat on the tarmac for about an hour and no one was allowed off. They announced that there was a problem. I began praying to St. Theresa for a safe flight. Finally we took off with our next stop being Chicago. I was heading for Ohio.

When we arrived in Chicago, beautiful hostesses greeted us with baskets of live red roses handing one to each passenger as we got off of the plane. I knew St. Theresa had heard and answered my prayers.

~Margaret - New Mexico

ROSES SENT WITH THE MESSAGE OF LOVE

My grandson, Gabriel, was having problems with stomach issues and enamel losses in his teeth. When Gabriel was 11 months old, he caught a virus that attacked his pancreas and he became a juvenile diabetic. The doctors were concerned he may have celiac disease. He had terrible stomach issues for a couple of months. I also prayed for his sister, Ariana, as she was only two years old and they were testing her for mononucleosis.

I had started my prayers before the children had their tests done. On March 30, 2003, my husband and I attended a 50th wedding anniversary for my sister and her husband. This day of the anniversary party happened to be the fifth day of my prayers to St. Therese. When my sister arrived, my nieces brought out two beautiful yellow, baby rosebud corsages for her and her husband.

When I saw the yellow baby roses, I caught my breath and said to myself, "Oh, my God." My husband also caught a glimpse of the beautiful rosebud corsages and later he told me that when he saw the 'roses' he felt a tingling go through his whole body and is was like "Wow!", those roses are special but he didn't know why.

Before we left, my sister came to me and hugged me and said, "I love you." She has never said that to me before. So you see, the *roses* were sent to me with a message of *love*.

On March 31, 2003, Gabriel's stomach issues were gone and about a week later my daughter got the test results back for both children and there was no Celiac disease or mononucleosis. I know without a doubt that St. Therese helped to get my prayers to God and brought the beautiful roses with a message of love to me on the 5th day of my prayers.

~Linda – Pennsylvania

IT'S THE LITTLE GIFTS

I n the early 1980's, my supervisor's husband was transferred to Wisconsin in his work. They had a lovely home in a desirable area that had to be sold. After several months and the house still had not sold, it was decided that the husband would move to Wisconsin and the wife would remain here until the desired sale. One Catholic friend said she should bury a statue of St. Joseph. Nothing happened. (There were no prayers involved.) Although the couple was not Catholic, they were getting very anxious so I told her about the 5-day novena to St Therese. She said, "Write down the prayers and I will say them." We agreed that I would pray them also, starting on

Monday morning at 7:00 a.m., explaining that if the answer were "yes" she would receive a rose.

The following Sunday was Mother's Day. On the Friday morning before, (the day the novena was completed) we each had a plastic rose on our desks! We were the only two that received roses. I worked in the mailroom and when we talked about this, there was no one around. The roses came from another employee who found joy in doing these little gifts just to surprise people.

The house sold the next week!

I am 81 years old and still remember the joy I felt when the sale was completed.

~Florence – Illinois

A YELLOW ROSE FOR LUNCH

In February of 1981 I had my first child, Jennifer, a beautiful daughter with Down Syndrome. We prayed to have another child, but after years of waiting, my doctor suggested we see a fertility doctor. We made an appointment, but in the meantime, I found a novena to St. Theresa in *Leaves Magazine*. I started the novena, asking for her intercession to conceive a child. On the ninth day, my husband came home from work and said he had something for me in his lunchbox. I opened the lunchbox and burst into tears. There was a beautiful yellow rose inside.

My husband, Greg, did not know I was saying the novena, in fact, he only became Catholic after we got married.

He was not used to praying to the saints for their help. I told him about St. Theresa and her promise. As a construction worker at the time, Greg was given a map to find an electrical utility pole in a new residential development. When he arrived at his destination, he got out of his truck and was surprised to see a beautiful rose laying there on the ground. He picked it up and put it in his lunchbox.

The next morning I called the fertility doctor and canceled my appointment. I knew I would get pregnant without his help. Nine months later I had a healthy, normal baby boy. And we named him Christopher.

When Christopher was a little over a year old, we started praying for another child. I received two roses from a friend who was thinking about me and decided to send me flowers. I found out that month that I was pregnant again. During the third month of my pregnancy, my husband and I were celebrating our anniversary and decided to go to the Poconos for the weekend. While we were away, my mom and dad were taking care of the children, thank God, because my husband and I were in a terrible car accident. My head went through the window and I needed stitches to my forehead and just above my eye. When we got to the hospital, my husband gave me my anniversary gift – a necklace of St. Theresa. The doctor at the hospital feared the baby would be affected from the trauma and suggested an abortion. Of course, I would not hear of it and on October 19, Kimberly Therese was born perfectly healthy and normal. She was confirmed on October 19th, her birthday, and the same day St. Theresa became a doctor of the Church.

So you see St. Theresa has been in our lives in a very special way!

~Marge – Pennsylvania

THE POWER OF A SINGLE ROSE

I n 1955, my mother, a person very devoted to St. Therese, had to have surgery for an abdominal hernia. The operation did not go well and resulted in several more intestinal obstructions. She had to undergo two more operations to correct this medical problem. There was a time when she was not expected to live.

We stormed Heaven with prayers to St. Therese for her recovery, even when it seemed impossible. Her doctor attached a relic of The Little Flower to her pillowcase.

One day, when my father was taking his daily walk down the immaculate hallway of the hospital to see my mother, he stopped to talk to the nurse that was taking care of her. She happened to look down at his shoe and told him that he was stepping on something. He moved his foot and discovered there was a rose under it. Remembering that a rose signified that St. Therese was listening and that she would be with you always, he knew his prayers had been answered.

He could hardly contain the joy he felt when he came home to tell me his wonderful news. I was 22 at the time and happy to say, both my mother and father lived to see me married in February 1957. They both passed away a couple of years later, but I was so thankful to St. Therese for allowing them to see me so content with the wonderful man I married.

~Delores- Florida

TEENAGER LEARNS THE POWER OF FAITH

My daughter, a teenager at the time, was looking for a summer job and I was praying the novena to St. Therese for her intervention.

One day my daughter, Cristol, was with her dad and they stopped for gas at our local station. My husband realized he didn't have his wallet with him and, because we lived close by, he walked home to get it.

Cristol stayed at the station to wait. While she was there, she asked if they needed summer help and was given an application. The next day, her boyfriend gave her a rose for no apparent reason. I knew the rose was St. Therese and that Cristol would get the job and she did. This incident helped my teen see the power of prayer and faith.

~Eileen – Ontario

SIMPLE EXCHANGE

I have always had great faith in St. Therese and she has bestowed so many favors on me and my loved ones. I am now 84 and my requests do not seem as frequent as in the past! However, I still pass on to my family and friends the little prayers to St. Theresa whenever a need surfaces – big or small.

St. Theresa, Little Flower, please pick me a rose from the Heavenly Garden and send it to me with a message of love. Ask God to grant me the favor I thee implore and tell Him I will love Him more and more.

I owned and operated a liquor store in Woodbury, Connecticut. I was alone in the store and saying my little prayer to St. Theresa, over and over. A gentleman walked into the store with a single red rose in his hand. He handed me the rose, gave me a big smile, and left. No purchase was made. No words exchanged! I did not know the man nor ever say him again! My request was answered!

~EllaRita – Connecticut

Chapter 4

Scent of St. Therese

"**R**emember that nothing is small in the eyes of God. Do all that you do with love."

~St. Therese

HEAVENLY FRAGRANCE

Thank you for giving me the opportunity to thank St. Therese publicly. I have wanted to do so for a long time.

In 1990, my husband was having pains in his jaw. Our family doctor advised him to have a stress test and quickly ordered another test, which showed blockage in four arteries.

During all of this time we were fervently praying to St. Therese. I had prayed to her for many years and encouraged my husband to do so, as well. Many cards sent from our family and friends had roses on them, although they were not aware of our devotion to St. Therese.

My husband's angioplasty surgery was scheduled for the following week. Before the surgery, a minister from the hospital (not of our faith) came to pray with him. As he finished, he gave my husband a prayer card with a big pink rose on the front. That's when we knew that St. Therese was working for us.

One night during his recuperation, my husband awoke to the scent of roses filling our bedroom. The next morning my husband asked if I had smelled the flowers in our bedroom the night before. I had not. We knew St. Therese had answered our prayers and he was going to be fine.

To this day, he has stress tests once a year and so far, thankfully, he has been okay.

We pray to St. Therese every day for his continued health and for our family.

~Berniece – Ohio

NO LONGER SKEPTICAL

About 30 years ago, I was facing a very serious kidney surgery. My neighbor came to my door and gave me a St. Therese card. She told me to say the novena that was printed on the back of the card and that St. Therese would take my petition to the Lord. My prayers would be answered with roses in some form. I was a weekly churchgoer but I surely did not believe that this was possible. I was very scared so I said the novena anyway.

A few days later I went to the hospital. On the way up to surgery, I was in a closed, empty elevator, when it was suddenly filled with the strongest, sweetest scent of roses. I was so happy! I knew that I would make it through the surgery.

They took off one-third of my kidney that contained a large kidney stone that was causing a lot of pain and bleeding. They sent the removed piece of kidney to the Mayo Clinic for testing.

A few days later my happiness bubble burst. The doctor came in with the Mayo's results. I had a serious disease and would need dialyses or a transplant soon. My mom had just died of this same disease at the age of 62. I cried, as I had five small children at home. I wondered how would they survive without their mom?

My roommate, a nun, said "Don't worry, tonight we will take it to the Supreme Court." That night she and another nun laid their hands on me and prayed. They started with "Lord, you have said if any of you are sick, call the elders of the church and the prayers of the faithful will save you." They prayed more, but after the above statement I just knew I was healed.

The doctors had me come back often to have my blood checked. Finally they said, "We don't understand it, we are not able to find any abnormalities, but come back when you have trouble." This was over 30 years ago. I had another baby girl, even though the doctors had warned me against having another child, but I had no difficulties.

~Marlene – Minnesota

THE CHURCH

t is hard to believe that there was ever a time when I had not heard about St. Therese and the roses. However, my rose experience started in the winter of 1976. My father had died and my mother had come to live with my husband, daughter, son and myself.

One Sunday morning during the winter, we left my mother at home and the four of us were going to mass at the Catholic Church in Utica, Michigan. I was walking on the sidewalk towards the stairs while some of the other churchgoers were already climbing the stairs and entering the church. I could distinctly smell roses. It was overwhelming. I asked them if they smelled roses, but they turned and looked down at me, concentrating on going up the stairs and getting into church. There was snow on the ground and not a green leaf to be seen. I looked all over, even went to the left of the staircase to see if there was a rose bush behind the stairs. No, there was not. I shrugged my shoulders and went into mass.

As you can imagine, I never forgot the incident. It was too unusual. Then, much later, I heard about how St. Therese answers prayers by sending roses or the scent of roses to people. And then I knew - it was she who sent the fragrance to comfort me to say that God was there to help me and that I was not alone.

~*Eileen – Florida*

SAFELY HOME

My dad always prayed to St. Therese, so when he was in the hospital with cancer, he was waiting for St. Therese to come and take him. My family was around him and everyone smelled roses, but there were none around and we believe that St. Therese came and brought him home.

When he passed, I asked St. Therese to send me yellow roses if my dad was okay. Well, the next day I went to church and guess what was around the Blessed Mother? Yes, yellow roses. Well, I thought I was going to faint. I was so happy!

I love that story and tell everyone. So now, every time I see a yellow rose, I know that dad is not far.

~*Mary Anne - New York*

ROSES AID IN RECOVERY

In 1981, when my 19 year old son was in the Army Paratroopers in North Carolina, a few of his friends wanted to go to the beach on a Sunday afternoon for a little rest and relaxation. When they arrived at the lake, they all jumped into the water. When my son jumped in, he hit his head on the bottom of the lake in very shallow water. He broke his neck and by the grace of God he was not paralyzed. The doctor said my son should have been paralyzed but he didn't why he wasn't – I knew why! We always prayed for him.

As I started my novena to St. Therese my son was going through some painful treatments. He was flown to Walter Reed Hospital to be operated on; a very serious operation which would take a few hours. My daughter and I decided to go out for a while and as I waited for my daughter in the lobby of the hospital, which was large and the flower shop quite small, the scent of roses was very strong. I thought St. Therese was answering my prayer. We then went to have lunch at a department store and upon opening the door found every counter decorated with artificial roses – eve the restaurant. I could not believe what I was seeing and knew then that St. Therese had listened and answered my prayer.

My son recovered and is a fine young man with a wife and four children. My husband and I are very grateful to God and St. Therese and continue our Novena every day.

~Doris – Florida

Chapter 5

Impressions of St. Therese

"Let us not be justices of the peace, but angels of peace."

~St. Therese

CONFIRMATION FROM HEAVEN

My husband suffered intensely for 15 years. The doctors at the Mayo Clinic called him a "red herring" as they could not find his problem and nothing they knew of could ease his unbearable pain. He would get on the floor and roll – his pain was so agonizing! He would sweat so much that you could wring out a bath towel that was drenched with his perspiration. The pain was so terrible that he would start throwing up and he just could not stop. He was in and out of the hospital all of the time. The last time I took him to the hospital, he folded his hands in prayer and begged me not to take him in.

He was in the Critical Care Unit for two months before he passed away. During this stay, he had two surgical procedures and what seemed like everything a person could possibly be put through. He was conscious till his very last breath. The night he passed away I sat by his bed and held his hand. All evening while holding his hand he never moved a finger. When he drew his last breath, he squeezed my hand and formed his lips to say "I love you" and he was gone. He died with a smile on his face.

Shortly after his passing, I prayed to St. Therese and asked her to send me a yellow rose if he was in heaven. A week later while I was watching TV, two, big, yellow roses appeared on the screen. I guess that was my answer.

~Phyllis – Michigan

MIRACULOUS HEALING

My mother wanted, and so did I, to have this story told long ago. My mother is now in Heaven but she will be very pleased to have you read it, as I am.

In 1927, I was born to a beautiful family only to have a deformity, a club foot, – one foot much shorter than the other. I could not run or skip with my brother and sister, but crept and stood on one foot. I was taken from doctor to doctor and the answer was always the same, "Your child will be crippled for life." At that time it was not operable. Mother would not accept this; her faith was too great.

A nine-day novena was started at our parish to St. Therese. Mother went every evening for the novena. She told St. Therese, "I give my little Therese to you. When you heal her, you can have her." On the ninth day, not only did my brother and sister run to my mother, but I did, too! I was completely cured! My mother's dream and prayers had been heard. Being healed, I was able to enter Nazareth. I persevered, making my profession and celebrating my 50th anniversary in Religious life. My mother at 92 years of age was present with my family, friends, and Sisters in religion who shared their love, kindness, concern, and caring for me.

~Sister Therese Marie, Sisters of the Holy Family of Nazareth – Pennsylvania

ROSES COME IN ALL FORMS

A few years ago my daughter applied for a good job close to their home. She was told that there were many applicants for the same job. I told her to say the novena to St.

Therese. Like me, she also did not believe, but a few days into the novena she called and said "Wow! I'm sure it doesn't mean anything, but I got a wooden jewelry box in the mail today and it has a rose on the top". I said, "Yes, it does mean something, you will get the job." and she did. She loves her new job along with her baby girl she had after seven years of marriage.

~Marlene – Minnesota

PRECIOUS ONES

My mother who passed away suddenly a few years ago, had great devotion to St. Therese, she was her favorite saint. I have a story I'd like to share with you.

I come from a large, by today's standards, Catholic family. My parents raised seven children, sent all of us to Catholic school and to college. I am the sixth child out of seven.

When I got married, it was my husband's and my dream to have children. We both loved children and I knew my husband would be an awesome father, because he raised his two younger sisters from age seven and nine, after his father passed away from cancer.

We tried for several years but with no success. Now this was in the 1970's when the infertility technology they now have did not exist yet.

I was fortunate to have a brother who was an OBGYN. He recommended we seek an infertility specialist in Detroit whom we were only able to get in to see because my brother had referred us. During this entire process I had two minor surgeries and one major surgery. During one of my surgeries it was discovered that I was born with only one fallopian tube and one ovary (which cut my chances of conception in half), I also had endometriosis.

After being under the specialists' care, taking fertility drugs for almost three years, and trying everything he knew, we were told our chances of having children we nil. We were devastated. I could not imagine life without children and adoption was not an option my husband was willing to consider.

My husband and I pursued our careers to fill the empty void. Holidays were always a challenge for me as we gather together as a family, playing with and seeing all my nieces and nephews while knowing I would never have children.

Many times I cried afterwards with pure envy. My mom NEVER gave up hope and never stopped praying for us! One day she called me and asked how I was feeling? She was concerned because I was just getting over my second bout of pneumonia that winter. I told her I was okay, just very, very tired. She suggested I visit my doctor and while I was there, to have a pregnancy test done. I was surprised to think she would even suggest this. "Mom, it's been nine years, the doctor's said we'd never have children." Then she told me her prayers had been answered. "Cathy, I have just finished another novena to St Therese, the Little Child, for you and I got my answer."

"Mom, what do you mean you got an answer?" "Roses!" she said, "I was in my chest of drawers. I just found a birthday gift I had not opened yet and when I did it was a beautiful sachet filled with the most beautiful scent of roses."

I went out the next day and purchased a home pregnancy kit. Well, it was negative. Ten days later, with no symptoms other than exhaustion, I purchased another home pregnancy test. My mom was right, I was pregnant!
My husband and I have two very wonderful young men and we couldn't be more proud of them. My mom always called my boys her "precious ones." She was right they are both precious gifts from God because of her prayers and the intervention of St. Therese, the Little Flower.

~Cathy – Michigan

SPECIAL FRIENDSHIP

I have a beautiful picture of St. Therese on my bedroom wall. I often "talk" to her like she's there in person. One day, a few years ago, I said to her, send me a sign that we are still friends. That's all I asked for. Well, about three or four weeks later, I received in the mail, a donation request from an organization that I contribute to. Also in the envelope was a card (not a greeting card) that had a small plastic charm in the middle of all roses. Around the charm is said, "A Rose of Friendship". I carry that card with me still.

~Maryann – Pennsylvania

FEARLESS FLIGHT

My daughter, Kelly, lives in Tucson, Arizona and we only get to see her at Christmas. Before she left for Arizona we were very close sharing many happy hours together, shopping, lunch dates, and talking frequently on the phone. So I was missing her very much and she, in turn, was missing me. Kelly asked me to come for a visit but I had never flown before. I have claustrophobia and can't take small spaces and crowds. Poor Kelly prayed to St. Therese for me to come out.

My older son Michael, who is a photographer, happened to be going to Arizona to photograph a program. Michael said if I would go to Arizona with him he would talk me through the plane ride. I purchased the airline tickets in advance with the thought – "If I didn't go, my husband would."

One day I would say "OK, I'll go" and the next day was "I can't do this!" I decided to say a novena to St. Therese, the Little Flower. If I should get on that plane, she would send me a pink rose. I asked that it be handed to me so there would be no mistake. After finishing the novena, I completely forgot about it.

A short time later, a little girl came to see me and handed me a small bag saying "Mommy said I had to hand this to you." It was a pin with a pretty pink rose on it. "Mom said we got this for you a month ago but couldn't find where it was. This morning it was on the table but we don't know how it got there!"

I started to put the pin on my blouse and remembered what I had asked for from St. Therese. I had to get on that plane. This was the first time I wasn't happy to receive my rose.

I got on the plane with my son and the whole time I kept praying that I wouldn't have an attack and need to get out of that plane for air. My son was wonderful, even holding my hand as we started to take off.

Unfortunately, the flight was over five hours long and at one point my son needed to use the rest room. While waiting for Michael to return, I started to panic and quickly said a prayer to St. Therese. "Please help me – you gave me the pink rose – so I'm supposed to be able to do this!"

I was almost in tears when someone tapped me on the back. As I turned to see who it was, a lady shoved something in my face. I wondered what she wanted. She was holding a pen out to me. She pointed to the pen and as I looked closer there was a pink rose on the pen. She smiled and continued to write on the tablet on her lap. She never said a word.

My son came back and we returned to our seats. It was then I realized St. Therese used that dear lady to remind me that she was with me and I had nothing to fear. I was perfectly calm and relaxed for the rest of flight.

My daughter came to the airport to pick up her brother. She had no idea that I had also made the trip. When she saw me, she jumped up and down and we both cried. Kelly said "Mom, I prayed to our dear friend, St. Therese to give you the courage to come here." We were both praying and St. Therese answered both of our prayers.

~Fay – Pennsylvania

SURGERY CANCELED

O ver 60 years ago, I received a miracle of health. Thanks to my mother who was making a novena to the Little Flower. As a child, I was very ill and one day the doctor who had come to check on me told his nurse to get me ready to go the hospital where I was to have surgery for a tracheotomy. My mother pleaded with the doctor to please take another look at me. To satisfy her, he took another look at me and the doctor then told the nurse, "we're not taking her to the hospital – she doesn't need surgery." Don't you consider that a miracle? For many days, I wasn't able to take medication or swallow. I also had a high fever that refused to come down. Needless to say, I pray the Little Flower Rosary Chaplet every day (over 60 years) in thanksgiving. I'm grateful for the gift of Faith.

~Maria – Wisconsin

MYSTERIOUS BEDSPREAD

I t was on March 3, 2001, when my husband couldn't get up from bed. He said, "I can't walk!" We rushed him to the hospital where he had a thorough examination. He was diagnosed with Guillain-Barre Syndrome. With his arms and legs paralyzed, he was in our local hospital for a month before being transferred to a nursing home for therapy.

He had both occupational therapy and regular therapy. After two weeks, the therapist told me that my husband wasn't responding at all. They also told me that Medicare would not pay for his therapy.

I prayed day and night for St. Therese to help him. He went back to occupational therapy, and the therapist there kept telling us that my husband couldn't do the exercises and felt that my husband would never improve.

Finally, after many prayers, I was feeding my husband and there, on his dinner tray, were two sugar packets with a picture of a rose on each. I cried because I knew that St. Therese would help him.

Two days later, I came into his room and started to cry again. On his bed was a bedspread with roses on it. When the nurse came into the room, she remarked that the bedspread I had brought for my husband's bed was very nice. I told her I wasn't the one who had brought it. The nurse replied that no one has a blanket like that on their bed. The next day, the bedspread was gone. Three days later, the spread came back. From that day he continued to improve. The occupational therapist said that after 15 years as a therapist, he had made a mistake in saying my husband would never improve.

After two more weeks of therapy, he was released from the nursing home. He went three times a week to our local hospital for more therapy. My husband was determined to walk. He passed away on January 6, 2008 but led a good life doing everything around our home, plus having a garden. He never gave up. Always say your prayers.

Gloria - New Jersey

SERENADED BY SAINT THERESE

It was a lovely, sunny day out in Montauk, the easternmost tip of Long Island, New York. Ron and I were on one of our earliest dates. We decided to stop and pray together inside the Church of St. Therese, the Little Flower.

Ron sat in a pew and cried out of joy that we had met. While he prayed, I circled the interior of the dark and empty church. I started to pray the rosary as I walked around. I too was thanking God for having brought Ron and I together.

After some time, we both heard about fifteen seconds of the Ave Maria play on the organ. However, there was absolutely no one but us inside the church. The choir loft was completely empty, and the organ was locked. Ron and I both knew that it was St. Therese playing the organ from heaven and we took this as a sign that we should marry! Now, fifteen years later, we can still remember the surprise of that heavenly favor.

~Marie - New York

NORTHWARD BOUND

After my husband died, I lived in Florida for a while, but I yearned to move back home to my home state in the north.

I asked the Little Flower to give me a sign of a yellow rose that she would do this for me.

She sent the sign of a yellow rose. Even though the rose was not a living rose, I knew it was an answer to my prayers and I was able to move back to Indiana.

~Vilma – Indiana

SCHOOL GRADES IMPROVE

This story was told to me by my daughter, Barb. Her daughter, Kelly was having trouble with her grades at school and she was much more interested in her dance lessons. My daughter was worried that Kelly, already being so tall, would be so much bigger than the rest of her classmates if she were held back another year.

So Barb prayed to St. Therese, "I have been praying to you for a long time. Help me with my daughter's school grades." She pleaded with St. Theresa to help her. Well, Kelly's marks got better and guess what? She came home from school, told her mother she would take St. Theresa's name for her confirmation name, out of the clear blue sky. Her mother was shocked. She couldn't thank St. Theresa enough.

~Helen – Pennsylvania

HEAVENLY VISION

This is back in the fifties. There were six of us girls applying for work and we had all taken a test and were told to come back at 2:00 in the afternoon. While I was waiting, I walked inside a church, sat down, and closed my eyes. I had seen a shadow (that was odd) that became a vision of a nun. I could see a crucifix in her hands and when the crucifix turned into roses, I knew it was St. Therese and she wants me to pray to her. I knew she had heard and answered my prayers as I got the job.

~Violet – Michigan

STRENGTH TO PERSEVERE

I t was in July 1952, a very hot and humid day. I was sitting in the living room with my three-month-old daughter who was born in April. It was a lonely, depressed day for me. My husband, who was an alcoholic, was out drinking again. Our house was very, very old and run down with no bathroom.

I placed my daughter in an old buggy and walked down the hill to my parent's house. I told them I wanted to leave my husband and move in with them. I couldn't tolerate my husband's drinking. My father definitely told me "NO." I was not going to raise my daughter without a father. I immediately started to cry.

Upon leaving to go back home, my sister came to me and gave me a prayer card. It was a prayer card and novena to St. Therese of Lisieux. She told me that if my prayer were answered, I would receive a rose.

I went home and right away started to pray the novena to St. Therese. A month later, in August of the year 1952, I was again sitting in my in my living room, lonely and depressed, so depressed that even though my daughter was crying in her bassinet, I was completely ignoring her.

There was a knock on my front door and when I went to answer, standing there were two nuns dressed all in white. They said they were Sisters of St. Paul of Pittsburg, selling religious books. When I asked the nuns if they might have a book of St. Therese, one reached into her habit and pulled out a book on the life of St. Therese. I purchased the book, and as they left my home, I watched them go up the street noticing that they did not stop at any other house. They walked and made a turn and disappeared.

I looked down at my daughter and she appeared to be calm and serene. I read the book and I loved it.

September of 1952, I was planning to leave my husband. He told me if I would stay, he would buy me a television set. I agreed. On September 30, 1952, the store delivered to my house a beautiful cabinet television. My relatives and friends came to my home and they were very excited for me and we chatted and visited.

That same day, as I was standing by the sink, washing dishes, a voice said to me, "Helen, go out on the front porch." As I was heading for the porch I looked at the clock. It was 7:20 p.m., the time and anniversary date of the day St. Therese died. It was a warm and beautiful fall night. I looked up at the sky and I saw rays of sunbeams shining down. I felt a great inspiration of love for God. I forgot all my troubles. I kept praising and thanking God. I felt so full of love. I felt the presence of St. Therese.

The next day I woke up and felt so energized and full of love. It helped me to get through my marriage. St. Therese was always with me. I had two more sons and I stayed in my marriage for 44 years until my husband died. I am now a widow. I have so many, stories to tell of St. Therese, so many miracles happened in my life through her.

~Helen - Pennsylvania

A MOTHER'S LOVE AND DEVOTION

In 1931, when I was 3 years old, I was severely burned and scalded from my shoulder to my buttocks when a steam valve broke open in our basement.

When our family doctor learned of this accident he told my parents that if I were hospitalized, the nursing staff would not be able to provide the constant care I would need in order to survive. So for the next fourteen weeks, my mom never left my side. She soaked towels in a solution of linseed oil and limewater. She applied them to the burned area of my left side continuously. The heat from my burn would dry the towels out almost immediately and she would apply another and another and another, day and night. She sat in a chair by my bed with little or no sleep the entire time.

Eventually, I was able to walk with a cane, however, after lying in bed for that many weeks, the skin on my left side and thigh had shriveled so terribly that I could not stand upright and the doctor had said that I might never be able to fully straighten my leg.

During this same period, my mother's cousin had been ordained in Rome. On his return, he brought a relic of St. Therese, the Little Flower, and gave it to my mom. She put the relic in my hand and said, "Little flower, use your power and help Joe to stand up". I immediately straightened and walked without the cane. Naturally, I have great devotion to the "Little Flower" and always pray to her and carry her relic. I truly consider myself to be one of her miracles.

~Joseph – Pennsylvania

CHANGE OF NAME

M y sister was born on October 3rd and my mother named her Linda. My aunt asked, "why are you naming her Linda when she was born so near St. Therese Day?" So my mother and father had her name and her birth certificate changed to Therese. It was a cute story and true. I just wanted to let you know.

~Mary Anne - New York

ROSES COME IN MANY FORMS

A bout a year ago, for nine days, I prayed the 24 Glory Be's in honor of St. Therese. I asked at the beginning for a white rose if my prayer was being heard. The very next day, in the mail, I received a picture of a white rose from my mother. On the 6th day, my prayer was answered.

I just started a novena to St. Therese yesterday. I've been trying to get a chaplet to St. Therese, but couldn't seem to find one. See with my being an inmate, everyone seems to think I am beyond Christian love. I've given my life over to the Lord and am trying to live a life according to God's will. I've made mistakes in my life and am paying for them. St.

Therese is my patron saint. I even have a rose petal that has been her relic.

~Jim – Texas

MIRACLE BIRTHS

n 1931, my mother, married for about 13 years, was having great difficulty in conceiving a child. The problem was endometriosis, a little known disease at the time.

In their neighborhood, it was common to have peddlers come to their door with suitcases filled with items to sell. My mother would always buy a little item to help them out. One day while conversing with the lady, she proceeded to tell her that she longed to have a child but was unable to conceive. The lady reached into her suitcase and gave her a small ring with a picture of St. Therese on it. My mother was told to wear the ring and it would bring her good luck.

The following year, in October of 1932, I was born and on the 3rd of that month, which was at the time, the feast day of St. Therese. I became their only child and was named Delores Therese. All throughout my school and working years, I always felt that St. Therese has been with me, guiding and helping me every day.

I met a wonderful man, Bill, that I married and we had a son, William, two years later. Then I began having the same difficulty in conceiving that my mother had. Eventually, I was told that I had an endometriosis problem and the chances of my ever having another child were very slim. I began calling on St. Therese to intercede and our daughter, Maureen Therese, was born five years later. The following year, I had to undergo a hysterectomy, which, of course, meant no more children. But St. Therese had already given me my two precious babies.

When our daughter was married in 1988, she discovered that she had inherited this disease in an advanced stage. Nobody ever thought that one day she would give birth to two beautiful children, a son, Shawn and a daughter, Haylee Therese.

Many roses have been sent to us throughout the years from the Little Saint that she said she "would send forth a shower of roses from Heaven." All these births have been, we feel, part of the shower of roses she promised and we feel honored to have her name included in ours.

~Delores – Florida

ADOPTION ON A VERY SPECIAL DAY

ach Francis was born December 31, 2003, and came into our home (brought from the hospital by my husband Bryan) on January 2, 2004, as a foster child. We were always in the process of adopting him, but had to wait for all the paperwork, etc. We were aware that anything could happen until finalization in court. But the many prayers and wonderful human services people more or less assured us that it was just a matter of time.

Well, we got a call asking if the date of Friday, October 1st would work! You can imagine my joy when I automatically connected that date with the feast of St. Therese! Also, it was about 9 months from birth – kind of like a pregnancy.

So on that Friday, Bryan Ezechial, (our three-year-old son and big brother to Zach), Zach and I went to the courthouse in Detroit Lakes, Minnesota to finalize our adoption of Zach Francis Olson.

We got pictures with the judge and our social worker. It was a short and simple procedure. Thanks be to God for the many people involved in Zach's adoption into our family – especially to his birth mother who chose to give him life.

~Barb – Minnesota

START OF A NEW CAREER

I had read about the five-day novena to St. Therese in *Leaves Magazine* many years ago, and decided to give it a try when I was trying to publish my book about hotels.

I tried five major publishers, all of whom sent me the usual letters of rejection. I had just about given up when I got the idea of sending the manuscript to a subsidy house and they accepted it. There was only one catch, it was going to cost me $3,150, which was more than I could afford. I decided to apply for a loan with a bank in New York. During this process, I was continually saying the novena to St. Therese. On the fifth day of the novena, I received a message to call Chemical Bank, the time that this message was left happened to be 11:00 a.m. This particular time of the morning is commonly known as St. Therese's Hour. My loan was approved and my book Mein Angry Host was the beginning of my career as a freelance writer.

~Eugene – Pennsylvania

ONE OF A KIND PILLOW

en years ago, I felt very sick and kept going to the hospital for tests. They couldn't seem to find anything wrong, yet I knew there was something very wrong.

I already had great faith in St. Therese, her novena, starts September 23, and ends on October 1st, which happens to be my birthday.

I decided to make the novena and ask St. Therese that the doctors would be able to find my trouble during the time I was praying the novena.

I was brought to the emergency room and they located the problem and I had surgery. They found out that I had colon cancer. After four days in the ICU, a nurse came to take me to a regular room so I could continue my recovery. She asked me if I have brought with me a pillow from home. I hadn't, but she said that the pillows that the hospital have do not have roses on them. I looked at the pillow and the material was full of roses! I was so excited, that I couldn't sleep all night as I was thanking St. Therese.

Today, I can tell you that I am totally healed. I have since lost my husband very suddenly and St. Therese continues to help see me through my loss.

~Viola – Canada

IT'S ALL ABOUT THE NAME

couple of years ago I started praying the St. Therese Rose Novena prayer for my nephew to find a nice girl to marry. I kept repeating the prayer daily before saying the rosary expecting to find or receive a rose, but noting came. I just kept saying the novena.

One day I went to visit my sister, my nephew's mother, and she said, "My son has met a girl and she is also Catholic." I replied, "That's nice, what is her name?" She said "Rose." I realized that I got my "rose"!

My nephew and Rose were married at St. Therese's Parish. During the wedding, they told the above story and presented me with a rose!

~Therese – Canada

AFTERLIFE MIRACLE

In 1982, I was living in West Yarmouth, Cape Cod. I was by myself except for my faithful poodle, Athena.

The previous Christmas, I had been introduced to a Carmelite Nun at our church's Christmas party. Her name was M. Carmel Cecelia. We became fast friends and the next thing I knew, she was sending me holy cards and gifts (statues of St. Therese, etc). She even invited me to go on a retreat to Canada with her prayer group. She literally "adopted" me at a time in my life that I needed "adopting." Little did she know, nor did anyone know, I had been having a recurring nightmare about my deceased sister Claire. In my dreams, I would see Claire with arms outstretched, pleading with me, having the same physical appearance she had when she died (haunting, emaciated, cancerous body). Morning after morning, I would wake up with tears streaming down my face. I never spoke of these nightmares to anyone.

In January of 1982, I was on unemployment having resigned (in protest) for the Division of Social Services. Sr. Celia was setting her self up as my advisor as I needed to launch a new position soon. She proceeded to urge me to make a novena to St. Therese, which I chose to ignore. By February, she was literally barraging me with more holy cards. She even sent me a beautiful afghan that was several shades of green, probably knitted by another elderly Carmelite nun. I thought to myself, "What on earth is this for?" I ended up using the afghan on my disabled mother's hospital bed that we had in the living room.

Sister Cecelia's idea of saying a novena was 27 days or prayer proceeded by a request to the Little Flower, St. Therese for a rose. "She always sends roses.", she said. I told Sister Cecelia that I hardly said my daily prayers let alone kneel down for 27 days, and after the "rose" comment, I told her that she'd been in the convent too long!

Needless to say, the end of February was fast approaching, I was still looking for a job and Sister was still pursing me. I finally said, "Okay Sister, I will make the novena, not because I believe, but because you believe."

That first night, the first week of March, I knelt down and remembering the promise of a rose, I prayed rather sarcastically. "Okay, St. Therese, Sister says that you send roses, so if you can send one rose, then you can send a dozen." I put my request in that St. Therese would help me find a job and I "ordered" the dozen roses, and to make it a little difficult, I wanted yellow roses, my favorite. Nightly, for 24 days I knelt and prayed the novena prayer followed by "pick me a rose from the Heavenly garden, 12 that is, and send them to me as a message of love."

On day 25, I was hired as a medical social work consultant by a private nursing agency in Cape Cod. This was an agency I had approached and convinced to hire me so that I could help them become certified by the Department of Public Health to provide Medicare and home care services. I was ecstatic.

The very next day, I was all set to call Sister Celia to tell her that I got a job. However, it had occurred to me that I didn't receive the roses that I had asked for from St. Therese. A little voice inside my head started saying, "What makes you think that St. Therese got you that job? You went to Cape Cod. You drew up the contract. You sold them the idea that they needed to hire you." "You, you, you." The devil started to move in on my prayer life and make me doubt my faith in St. Therese.

Early in the morning on the 27th day of the novena, something powerful intervened. I was startled awake by a loud knocking on my sliding glass door. These doors lead out to a small garden. I got up out of bed and pulled back the curtains to see who was there. In front of me was a vision of my deceased sister Claire. She was very radiant and wearing a long, very bright, white gown tied with a brown sash. I remember staring in disbelief, tracing her features from head to toe. Her face was full and pink and she showed no sign of the cancer that took her life. I couldn't take my eyes off of her, I watched every gesture, and she turned towards the door and began to approach me. As I looked down, in her arms, she was holding the dozen yellow roses I had been praying for. They were stunning. She lifted the roses and then disappeared. I like to call this my "Healing Dream." My nightmares ceased. I know St. Therese and Jesus healed me.

~Mary – Massachusetts

5-DAY NOVENA TO ST. THERESE

St. Therese promised that she would shower roses from Heaven after her death. She also promised that those who prayed to her would always receive an answer. Her intercessory prayer is very powerful before the throne of God.

The following is the 5-day novena to St. Therese

Recite this prayer: "St. Therese, the Little Flower, please pick me a rose from the heavenly garden and send it to me with a message of love. Ask God to grant me the favor I thee implore and tell him I will love him each day more and more."

Recite the above prayer plus 5 Our Father's, 5 Hail Mary's, and 5 Glory Be's each day.

They must be said on 5 successive days, before 11 a.m.

On the 5th day the 5th set of prayers having been completed, offer one more set of 5 Our Father's, 5 Hail Mary's and 5 Glory Be's.

Pray with Confidence. Try to say it the same time every day so you don't forget. If you don't receive a rose by the 5th day, don't be discouraged. St. Therese is always listening and will answer you in God's Time. Continue with perseverance.

This prayer is not "magic". It is a spiritual devotion to help draw us closer to Jesus through the intercession of St. Therese.

Remember, we don't always get what we ask for. We receive from the Lord and His Father what is *best for us*. So pray with faith knowing you are being upheld and caressed.

It is my desire to continue to spread the word about St. Therese and her intercessions.

If you have a story you would like to share, please feel free to send it to me at the address listed below. I am hopeful to receive enough stories to put together another book in the future.

To order more copies of this book for family and friends, please visit www.amazon.com, or www.lulu.com, or by mail, write to this address:

Rebecca Fabiano
3292 Meadow Glenn Dr.
Hudsonville, MI 49426